Help Me Understand

What Happens When My Parent Dies?

Melissa Raé Shofner

PowerKiDS press

NEW YORK

Published in 2019 by The Rosen Publishing Group, Inc.
29 East 21st Street, New York, NY 10010

First Edition

Editor: Elizabeth Krajnik
Book Design: Rachel Rising

Photo Credits: Cover patat/Shutterstock.com; p. 4 Maria Maarbes/Shutterstock.com; p. 5 MK photograp55/Shutterstock.com; p. 6 favorita1987/Shutterstock.com; p. 7 Westend61/Getty Images; p. 9 Andrey_Popov/Shutterstock.com; p. 11 RubberBall Productions/Brand X Pictures/Getty Images; p.12 © iStockphoto.com/digitalskillet; p. 13 Torgado/Shutterstock.com; p. 15 Alena Ozerova/Shutterstock.com; p. 16 Ruslan Guzov/Shutterstock.com; p. 17 DGLimages/Shutterstock.com; p. 19 Monkey Business Images/Shutterstock.com; p. 21 Sladic/Shutterstock.com; p. 22 Sergiy Bykhunenko/Shutterstock.com.

Cataloging-in-Publication Data

Names: Shofner, Melissa Raé.
Title: What happens when my parent dies? / Melissa Raé Shofner.
Description: New York : PowerKids Press, 2019. | Series: Help me understand | Includes glossary and index.
Identifiers: LCCN ISBN 9781508167044 (pbk.) | ISBN 9781508167020 (library bound) | ISBN 9781508167051 (6 pack)
Subjects: LCSH: Children and death–Juvenile literature. | Bereavement in children–Juvenile literature. | Grief in children–Juvenile literature. | Parents–Death–Psychological aspects–Juvenile literature.
Classification: LCC BF723.D3 S56 2019 | DDC 155.9'37083–dc23

Manufactured in the United States of America

CPSIA Compliance Information: Batch #CS18PK: For Further Information contact Rosen Publishing, New York, New York at 1-800-237-9932

Contents

Losing a Parent

All living things will die someday, but knowing this doesn't make losing a loved one any easier. Dealing with the death of a parent is very hard. It can be a **confusing** time filled with strong feelings and many changes.

No matter what happens, know that you're not alone. There are people in your life who love you and will take care of you. It may take a long time to feel better, but everything will be OK.

You may be very sad after your mother or father dies. Just remember that you're not alone. There are people in your life who love you.

5

Many Different Feelings

Your parent's death may leave you feeling confused. You might not understand what's happening or why. At first, it might be hard to think about your parent really being gone. You might also feel angry and wonder why this would happen to your family. All these feelings are **normal** and OK.

You might feel **guilty** about your parent's death. But you're not to blame! Death isn't something we can control. There are many reasons it happens, but none of them are because of you.

Sharing your feelings with someone you trust, such as a friend or a family member, might help you feel better.

7

Grieving

Great sadness after someone dies is called grief. When you're feeling or showing grief, it's called grieving. This is sometimes also called mourning. Everyone grieves in their own way and for different amounts of time. You might grieve for a long time, but know that you won't feel sad forever.

For a while, you might have trouble sleeping, eating, or paying attention in school. This is normal, but you should talk to an adult about it. You need to take care of yourself, even when you're sad.

Therapists are special doctors who can help you while you grieve. You can talk to a therapist one on one or in a group—whichever feels better to you.

The Funeral

Soon after your parent's death, your family might have a funeral for them. A funeral is a special service held for someone who has died. It's a chance for the people who loved your parent to say goodbye and grieve together.

A funeral might feel like a sad event, but it's also a time to remember your parent and honor their life. Your family and your parent's friends may also gather after the funeral to eat, talk, and share **memories**.

People often say things such as "I'm sorry for your loss" after someone you love dies. It may be hard to hear this again and again, but people are just showing you they care.

11

Dealing with Fear

Death can happen for many reasons. Your parent may have been sick, or they may have been in an **accident**. You may be afraid that your other parent may also become sick or get in an accident. Feeling sad and afraid is normal, but worrying all the time isn't healthy.

Remember, there are many people in your life who **support** and care for you. If you're feeling afraid, talking to a trusted adult about your fears can help you feel better.

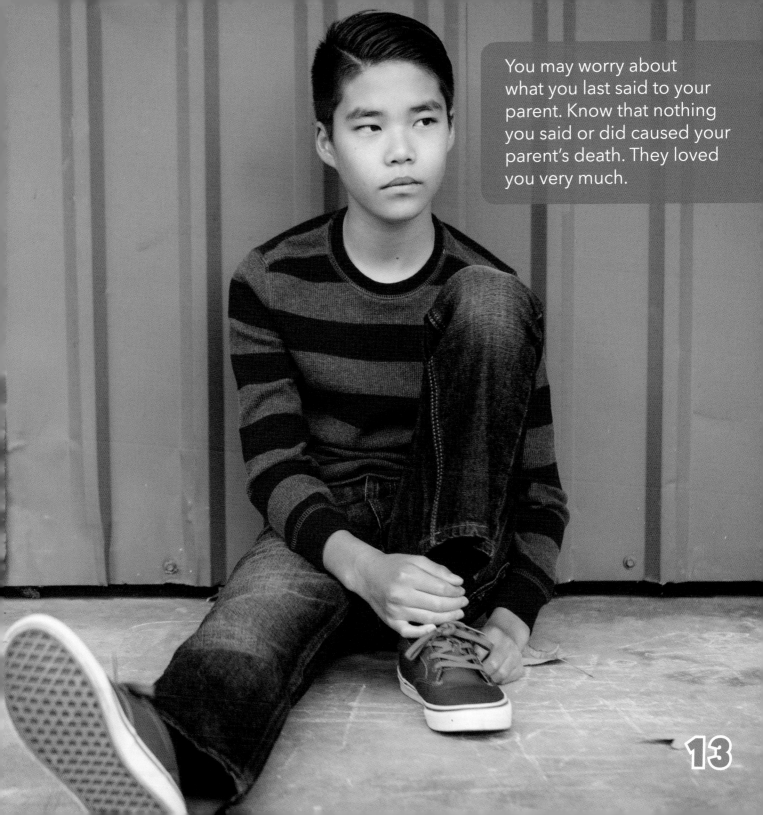

You may worry about what you last said to your parent. Know that nothing you said or did caused your parent's death. They loved you very much.

13

Let Love In

Losing someone you love, such as your mom or dad, can be very painful. After their death, you might find yourself pushing away the people who are closest to you. You might be afraid to love them for fear they may also die.

Even though you may be afraid, you shouldn't shut out the people you love. Your family and friends want to help you feel better. You need them now more than ever. Shutting them out may make you feel even sadder.

Other people in your family are dealing with the death of your parent, too. Spending time with the people you love can help everyone grieve.

→

15

Changes at Home

After the death of a parent, there will be many changes around your home. Your mom or dad may need to work more to support your family. Another family member, such as a grandparent, might spend more time with you for a while until things settle down.

Even though you may be sad or upset, your family might need you to help out around the house more. This will make life easier for everyone during this hard time.

Helping out around the house might also help you feel better after the death of a parent. It's important to grieve, but it's also good to stay busy.

17

In Time

You may be sad for a very long time after your mom or dad dies. It might feel like you'll never be happy again. In time, however, you'll begin to feel better. Take as much time as you need to grieve. When you're ready, your sadness will start to fade.

Know that your parent would want you to be happy. You'll always miss your mom or dad, but someday you'll be able to think of them and smile instead of cry.

You may be very upset about losing your mom or dad, but it's OK to play with your friends when you're ready. Your parent would want you to have fun.

Good Memories

It can take months or even years for your sadness to fade after your parent dies. Understand that it's OK to feel better. It doesn't mean you're forgetting about your mom or dad. They'll always be with you in your heart and your memories.

Holidays can be hard without your parent around, but remember that they'd want you to be happy. You can enjoy the holiday and honor your parent by keeping their favorite holiday **traditions** alive.

Did you and your parent make special foods or listen to certain music for holidays? Continuing to practice these traditions can help you remember good times spent with your mom or dad.

Coping with Death

Dealing with the death of a parent isn't easy. You may grieve for a long time and feel like you'll never be happy again. Your parent would want you to be happy and, in time, you'll feel better.

It can be hard to get used to life without your mom or dad. Your family members may also be very sad, but know that they love you and care for you very much. Together, you'll make it through this hard time.

Glossary

accident: An unexpected and sometimes bad event.

confusing: Hard to understand.

guilty: Feeling that you have done something wrong.

memory: Something that you remember.

normal: Usual, not strange.

support: To care for and help.

tradition: A way of thinking, behaving, or doing something that's been used by people in a particular family for a long time.

Index

Websites

Due to the changing nature of Internet links, PowerKids Press has developed an online list of websites related to the subject of this book. This site is updated regularly. Please use this link to access the list: www.powerkidslinks.com/help/death